LINDISFARNE CASTLE

Northumberland

THE NATIONAL TRUST

Acknowledgements

This new guidebook draws on that written in 1978 by Peter Orde, who was assisted by the then Historic Buildings Representative for Northumbria, Sheila Pettit, and revised in 1986 by her successor, Roger Carr-Whitworth. It also incorporates ideas from Colin Amery's colour souvenir. Lytton Strachey's letter describing a visit to Lindisfarne is in the Harry Ransom Humanities Research Center, University of Texas at Austin, and is quoted by kind permission of the Society of Authors as agents of the Strachey Trust. The National Trust is also grateful to Jane Ridley for her help with Lutyens's letters and to Dr Michael Tooley, formerly of the University of Durham, for additional information on Gertrude Jekyll's designs for the Walled Garden, which are now in the Reef Point Collection, University of California at Berkeley. The Walled Garden has been re-created as far as possible in accordance with these designs, in consultation with Richard Bisgrove.

Oliver Garnett, 1999

Due to recent research and renovation some items of the collection are not situated in the positions indicated in this guide.

Photographs: British Architectural Library/RIBA, London p. 36; BAL/RIBA, London/Jane Ridley p. 18 (bottom right); BFI Films: Stills, Posters and Designs/Odyssey Video p. 45; British Library p. 26; Country Life Picture Library pp. 4 (bottom left), 5, 41; Hunterian Art Gallery, University of Glasgow, Mackintosh collection p. 33; Tyne and Wear Museums p. 31; National Portrait Gallery, London p. 24; National Trust pp. 13, 18 (top left), 30, 37 (top), 42, 44; NT/Viscount Ridley p. 4 (bottom right); National Trust Photographic Library p. 38 (bottom); NTPL/A. C. Cooper p. 27; NTPL/Jenny McMillan pp. 22; NTPL/Joe Cornish front cover, pp. 6–7, 25, 34–5, 46–7; NTPL/Andreas von Einsiedel pp. 1, 9, 10, 11, 12, 14, 15, 16, 17, 19, 20, 21, 28, 38 (top), 39, back cover; NTPL/Charlie Waite pp. 23 (top and bottom), 37 (bottom), 40; Public Record Office p. 32; Tate Gallery, London p. 43.

Registered charity no. 20584

ISBN 1-84359-117-0

Reprinted 2001, 2002, 2005; revised 2004

Designed and typeset from disc by James Shurmer (4.01.05)

Print management by Astron for the National Trust (Enterprises) Ltd, 36 Queen Anne's Gate, London SW1H 9AS

(*Front cover*) Lindisfarne Castle from the west

(*Title-page*) The model of the Dutch merchantman *Henrietta* after which the Ship Room is named

(*Back cover*) The Dining Room

CONTENTS

LINDISFARNE CASTLE

From Tudor Fortress to Holiday Home

From 1902 the architect Edwin Lutyens turned the derelict Lindisfarne Castle into a holiday home for his friend and patron, Edward Hudson. So Lindisfarne is an Edwardian house, but it stands on an island hallowed for fourteen centuries.

A HOLY ISLAND

In AD 635 the Irish evangelist St Aidan founded a community of monks here, which became one of the most important centres of Christianity in Anglo-Saxon England. He was soon followed by St Cuthbert, in whose memory the Benedictine monks rebuilt the Priory in 1082 and renamed the place Holy Island.

KEEPING OUT THE SCOTS

In Tudor times, Holy Island occupied a key position near the unruly Scottish border. Lord Hertford recognised its importance in 1543, when he landed over 2,000 soldiers on the island on his way north to subdue the Scots. Fortifications were tried on various parts of the island, but the most enduring were on Beblowe Crag. The fortress of 1570–2 is still the basis of today's castle.

Edward Hudson

Edwin Lutyens

DECLINE

The accession of James VI of Scotland to the throne of England in 1603 united the two kingdoms, and Lindisfarne Castle lost its role as a border fort. However, for the next three centuries the Berwick garrison maintained it to defend the Holy Island harbour. Latterly, it served as a coastguard station.

AN EDWARDIAN HOLIDAY HOME

Edward Hudson, the founder of *Country Life* magazine, discovered the neglected remains of the empty castle in 1901. At once he realised its potential. Lutyens was Hudson's favourite architect, and as a romantic he responded with equal enthusiasm to the challenge of making a new home inside the old castle. He created austere, but beautifully designed interiors, linked by dramatic corridors, galleries and stairways. The austerity was tempered with whitewashed walls, patterned brick floors, shiny brass, old carpets, blue-and-white china and good, honest furniture. Both Hudson and Lutyens loved the quiet atmosphere of Dutch seventeenth-century interiors, and commissioned a series of photographs of Lutyens's children at Lindisfarne that powerfully recall the world of Vermeer's paintings.

Hudson enjoyed playing host to summer parties for friends and distinguished visitors, who included the future George V and Queen Mary in 1908. He never married, and in 1921 sold the castle, with most of its contents, to a London stockbroker, Oswald Falk. He in turn sold it to a banker, Sir Edward de Stein, who gave it to the National Trust in 1944 as its first twentieth-century house.

(Right) Barbie Lutyens in the Kitchen in 1910
(Overleaf) Lindisfarne Castle from the south

TOUR OF THE CASTLE

The Interior

THE ENTRANCE HALL

Lutyens loved to dramatise the routes through his houses. The Entrance Hall is one of the most complex spaces he created at Lindisfarne. The sturdy columns and rounded arches divide the room into three and recall in miniature the great Norman nave of Durham Cathedral. The single column on the right, carrying two arches, has an octagonal capital, in contrast to the two plainer columns on the left, which support three arches. None has a base – a Lutyens innovation: the sandstone shafts rise from the flagstones like tree-trunks from grass.

WIND INDICATOR

Above the fireplace is a wind indicator, painted in 1912 by Macdonald Gill, a younger brother of the sculptor Eric Gill. In the centre is a map of Holy Island. Around it, the defeated Spanish Armada is being pursued by the English fleet across the North Sea in August 1588 past Lindisfarne and the other castles that protected Northumberland. Lutyens often incorporated such indoor weathervanes into his houses, perhaps remembering how his Dutch ancestors had used such indicators to estimate when their ships might come in.

PICTURE

On the right-hand wall is a portrait of Edwin Lutyens as a boy, painted in the 1870s by his father Charles Lutyens (1829–1915), a soldier who became a professional animal painter.

FURNITURE

The iron-bound oak coffer with domed lid under the window is sixteenth-century Flemish.

The wide seventeenth-century oak court cupboard against the left-hand wall once had a third section on top that was used as a plate rack. The Flemish clock is seventeenth-century.

The carved oak figures with flat backs in the fireplace are thought to have originally been church pewends, *c.* 1700.

CERAMICS

The ginger jars are Chinese, *c.*1900.

TEXTILES

The tapestry on the wall opposite the entrance door is seventeenth-century and probably Flemish. The subject is uncertain, but may show a king receiving tribute or the judgement of Solomon.

WEAPONS

The halberds are a reminder that Lindisfarne was originally built to be defended.

HERALDRY

The hatchments, or achievements of arms, feature the royal arms of Spain and Portugal, possibly including those of Philip II, who launched the Spanish Armada.

The door by the clock leads into the Kitchen.

THE KITCHEN

Even the Kitchen is spartan, with pale wooden furniture, white plaster walls and grey stone floor. Lutyens placed the coal-fired range within a surprisingly wide stone fireplace, the scale of which adds a new dimension to a relatively small room. He often played with effects of contrasting scale in his designs for the castle.

(Right) Lutyens's new Entrance Hall recalls the nave of Durham Cathedral in miniature

FURNITURE

To the left of the range is an early nineteenth-century settle in elm, with a high curved back and drawers under the seat. The cupboard in the back was used for hanging bacon.

On the opposite side of the fireplace is the oak dresser designed for the room by Lutyens, who even devised the characteristically simple handles. There are similar examples throughout the castle.

The wall clock is eighteenth-century, from Friesland in Holland. Its origins and maritime decoration must have appealed to Lutyens: the pendulum mechanism tosses sailing ships on a choppy sea.

METALWORK

Around the fireplace is a collection of copper and pewter cooking pots, some of which were designed by W. A. S. Benson, one of the pioneers of Arts and Crafts metalwork. The best are perhaps the fish-kettles, which are embossed with scaly fishes on their covers.

THE SCULLERY

The Scullery must have been a cramped and somewhat draughty place to work. It contains not only the expected sink and wooden draining racks, but also, opposite the window, the winding gear and weights for operating the portcullis over the entrance door to the Lower Battery. Lutyens made sure that Lindisfarne remained a working castle.

Return to the Entrance Hall. Through the doorway opposite the entrance door a stepped passage leads to the Dining Room (on the right).

The Scullery.
The overhead wires
operate the portcullis

(Left)
Lutyens designed the
dresser to the right of
the fireplace in the
Kitchen

THE DINING ROOM

You are now back inside the old Tudor fortress. This and the Ship Room at the end of the passage were vaulted to take the weight of the cannons on the battery above, and served as the fort's gunpowder magazines. As a reminder of the past, Lutyens inserted the neo-Gothic traceried windows, and to make sure that the reference was not hidden, he hung the window curtains on special rods that swing out against the side walls of the recess.

The Dining Room has a wide-arched chimneypiece at the far end, which conceals an old bread oven within it: the room had earlier served as a bakery. The dourness of the enveloping stonework is relieved by the Prussian blue of the end wall and by the floor, which is laid with red bricks in the herringbone pattern that Lutyens loved.

Here Hudson would entertain his guests with lobsters and large quantities of champagne. Drink got the better of one guest 'with a voice like a megaphone and an infinite heartiness', according to the writer Lytton Strachey, who was staying here in September 1918:

Carried away by exhilaration, he made a speech – a long, long speech, proposing the health of 'our host' in heartfelt sentences – one sat gasping – the unimaginable farrago seemed to last interminably ... Hudson found himself replying, at equal length, and with an even wilder inconsequence.

Lutyens designed the table specially for the Dining Room. The old ceiling was vaulted to take the weight of the cannons once on the battery above

Linda Lilburn, the de Steins' housekeeper, in the Dining Room

FURNITURE

Lutyens designed the oval dining-table specially for the room. The Windsor chairs were made in the eighteenth century, and the walnut side-table is Italian.

METALWORK

The brass chandelier is seventeenth-century Dutch. The fireplace contains more examples of Benson copper-work. The two lidded pewter tankards are seventeenth-century.

Walk further down the passage to the Ship Room.

THE SHIP ROOM

The room takes its name from the wooden model that hangs from the barrel vault – the *Henrietta* of Amsterdam, a three-masted merchantman of the 1840s. The idea may again have been inspired by Lutyens's Dutch seafaring ancestors. Appropriately, it is flanked by two Dutch seventeenth-century chandeliers, which came from Deanery Garden, the house Lutyens had built for Hudson in Berkshire.

Lutyens designed the chimneypiece, which makes magnificent use of the end wall, but was not very practical, often filling the room with smoke, when the wind was blowing. The archway to its right leads to a little room used for storing logs.

Lutyens was also responsible for the special back cradles in which kindling was carried up to the castle.

The relatively small, delicately detailed windows are in contrast to the massive openings which contain them, and again show Lutyens in Gothic mood.

FURNITURE

The simple Dutch Rococo china cabinet against the wall facing the fireplace is painted with marbled mouldings and with scenes of peasant life on the lower doors. Above it hangs a carved wood achievement of arms of George I. The English oak gate-leg table and the Flemish walnut writing-table both date from the seventeenth century. The room also contains a set of five typical Charles II period walnut chairs.

CERAMICS

The yellow earthenware vases on the table opposite the windows belonged to Oswald Falk, who bought the castle from Hudson in 1921. They bear the royal yacht cipher and have been converted into electric lamps. On the facing table is a continental faience tankard with pewter mount.

Return along the passage, go upstairs to the gallery level, and turn right. Walk along the passage, and then left into the East Bedroom.

The Dutch cabinet in the Ship Room is painted with scenes of seventeenth-century peasant life

Lutyens inserted the fireplace and windows into one of the gunpowder magazines of the old fort to create the Ship Room

The East Bedroom is filled with the plain furniture that Hudson favoured, including a long table and little wall cabinets designed by Lutyens

THE EAST BEDROOM

Hudson's most important guests probably slept here, as this is the largest and most sheltered of the bedrooms. The fireplace shows once again Lutyens's fondness for playing with scale: the massive stone lintel dwarfs the red-brick fire-surround below.

FURNITURE

The oak four-poster bed was made in Flanders in 1753 and is one of two in the castle. Lutyens designed the little cupboards hanging on the walls and the long table under the window, which is so large that it must have been assembled in the room. Such a table would normally be found in a dining-room rather than a bedroom, suggesting that it may have been used for dinner parties that were too large for the Dining Room. Standing on the table is a carved and gilt Italian dressing mirror. Also continental is the eighteenth-century burr elm cabinet.

PICTURES

Over the fireplace hang a reproduction of Augustus John's 1917 portrait of Lutyens (now at Blagdon Hall) and three sepia watercolours of ships.

PHOTOGRAPHS

The photographs on the table include atmospheric images of Lutyens's children, Barbara and Robert, taken while they were staying in the castle in 1910. They show very well the kind of visual effect that Lutyens was aiming at – walls bare, the floors brick or painted, just a few isolated objects – a harpsichord or a birdcage. These photographs make the interiors of the castle look like paintings by Vermeer – calm and domestic and a secure refuge from the storms of life.

There is also a portrait of Lutyens's frequent collaborator, Gertrude Jekyll, who designed the planting for the Walled Garden, which you can see from the window.

CARPET

The Indian carpet is a modern substitute; the yellowed off-white painting of the floor surround follows Lutyens's original.

Return to the passage and climb five steps to the Long Gallery.

THE LONG GALLERY

This is one of the few completely new spaces Lutyens created in the castle, intended to link the former Commander's Lodging on the Upper Battery with the old garrison barracks. With the row of bedrooms along the north side, it covers the original Royal Battery. Again, stone, dark wooden beams, whitewashed plaster and red brick laid in herringbone pattern were the materials used. From the window seats you can look out on to the Upper Battery; the curtains are once more hung on hinged rods.

At the near end of the gallery two round stone arches springing from the same point divide the

Lutyens built the Long Gallery to connect the row of new bedrooms with the living rooms downstairs. Hudson's guests would gather here in the evenings for music and conversation

Barbie Lutyens looking down into the stairwell.
Lutyens loved to dramatise the passages and stairways in
his houses

stairs from the bedroom gallery passage. At the far end a large stone archway creates a cosy corner with a fireplace. Hudson's initials 'EH' and the date 1906 (when Lutyens's work was completed) appear on the cast-iron fireback.

FURNITURE

Beyond the windows on the left is an unusual piece of sixteenth-century furniture. Known as an aumbry, it is an upright cupboard, probably from a Dutch church, with decorative linenfold carving, which resembles stiffly folded cloth. It was intended for storing and washing vessels used in worship.

The solid walnut Flemish refectory table against the right-hand wall is 3.3 metres long and dates from the seventeenth century.

PICTURES

The engravings include a series of hunting scenes by Johann Elias Ridinger and two prints after the great German Renaissance artist Albrecht Dürer in elaborate giltwood frames.

Off the gallery, side-by-side, are the two North Bedrooms. On the right is the North-East Bedroom.

THE NORTH-EAST BEDROOM

The detailing of the doors and beam ends shows how passionate Lutyens was to maintain the standard of traditional craftsmanship in his buildings. The floor has been repainted in a shade of green as near as possible to the original.

FURNITURE

The fine eighteenth-century marquetry bed is Flemish.

The mahogany washstand was made in England in the early nineteenth century and is fitted with a blue-and-white slop bowl and soap dish. Even when Hudson was entertaining house parties here, there was only one bathroom. Maids were kept busy running along the cold stone passages with jugs of hot water, filling up the hip baths placed by the log fires in the bedrooms.

The chairs are part of a set of six, inlaid with marquetry and with lyre-shaped backs, of the French *Directoire* period, dating from about 1810.

Hudson, Lutyens and his daughter Barbie going to bed; a sketch by Lutyens

The North-East Bedroom

THE NORTH-WEST BEDROOM

FURNITURE

The four-poster bed is Flemish, apparently dating from the seventeenth century, although it bears the date 1807. It has a carved and panelled oak head, and cupboards at the foot and head of the bed, traditionally used to hold firearms. Here, they were more probably filled with nightcaps, knitting, bedsocks and good books.

Return to the Long Gallery and walk to the far end, where a door on the left under a very low arch (MIND YOUR HEAD) leads to the West Bedroom.

THE WEST BEDROOM

Painted letters on the door (now hidden by later paint) reveal that this room once served as the magazine for storing gunpowder. Now, like all the bedrooms, this is a whitewashed, somewhat monkish cell. Hudson placed very large beds in these rooms, which – paradoxically – help to magnify the space.

FURNITURE

The Dutch seventeenth-century carved and panelled oak bed stands on a raised platform. The upper section of the bed-head contains a cupboard with a sliding door. Below is an obscure inscription in Dutch beneath a carved bird: ANN MARIE ENGELBOTT ERBIJS OM AIJ EDERFALS, apparently celebrating the marriage of Anne Mari and Engelbott.

The chest-of-drawers is mid-seventeenth-century.

To the left of the archway near the end of the Long Gallery, steps lead upwards to another room, originally a bedroom, but now shown as an upper gallery.

THE UPPER GALLERY

This long, low, narrow room is the highest in the castle. It has a platform at one end and a bow window at the other, overlooking the village and the mainland beyond. The floorboards are again painted, in a cloudy blue.

The cello is a reminder that the room was used by Madame Suggia, a flamboyant cellist and friend of Edward Hudson, who was a regular visitor to Lindisfarne. Here she would practise Bach suites for hours on the Stradivarius Hudson gave her (not the instrument shown here).

FURNITURE

The furniture is mainly English oak, and includes a Charles II chest-of-drawers inlaid with mother-of-pearl and ivory, a set of early nineteenth-century spindle-back chairs (sometimes called 'Lancashire' chairs), and a Flemish marquetry fall-front bureau of the eighteenth century. At the platform end is an unusually shaped oak corner cupboard.

The West Bedroom

*The Upper Gallery, where Hudson's friend, the cellist
Mme Suggia, would play Bach suites to his guests*

The Exterior

PICTURES

The engravings include an eighteenth-century
coloured set of portraits, mainly of Italian artists
(eight more are in the bedrooms), and a set de-
picting silk farming and weaving as it was carried
out in one of the great Florentine houses of
the sixteenth century. These were engraved by
Philip Galle (1537–1612) after the originals by Jan
Stradanus (1523–1605).

*Before leaving the castle, you can enjoy fine views from
the Upper Battery.*

THE UPPER BATTERY

From here you can see the harbour and the ruins
of the Priory, the Farne Islands (which are also in
the care of the National Trust) and the shallow
curve of sand beach ending at Bamburgh Castle, as
well as the low outlines of sandbanks and mud-
flats, which have trapped many unwary sailors.
On the battery itself is the emplacement for a rifled
64-pounder muzzle-loading gun installed in 1882
as part of the castle's last armament, and removed
in 1893.

21

The castle from the north. The Upper Battery is on the right

LIME QUARRYING

The slender obelisks on Old Law on the mainland opposite the castle were originally designed by John Dobson for Trinity House as navigation aids for ships using Holy Island harbour. Lime had been quarried and burnt on the island since the eighteenth century, but in about 1860 a Dundee company began to operate on a commercial scale, building a battery of kilns immediately east of Beblowe Crag. These were last used in about 1900.

The jetty which served the company's ships is now represented by a few gaunt timbers jutting from the sea at the beach near the gate to the castle field. The tramway embankments which carried the lime to the kilns have long been grassed over, but the kilns with their fine stone vaulting still exist as a monument to the high standard of industrial building over a century ago.

To leave the castle, return down the stairs to the Entrance Hall and walk out on to the Lower Battery.

THE LOWER BATTERY

Although this no longer has the cannon for which it was planned, there are still two granite emplacements for rifled muzzle-loading guns used between 1882 and 1893 by the Volunteer Coast Artillery detachment. The Lower Battery also still offers much the same sweeping views of sea and land – from Berwick-on-Tweed in the north to Bamburgh Castle in the south – as the castle's soldiers enjoyed 400 years ago.

Walk down the covered steps to a small vestibule with arched recesses containing curved wooden seats.

THE RAMP

The stone ramp is laid with cobbles in a herringbone pattern – a familiar Lutyens touch. Lutyens removed the parapet wall from the ramp in order to increase the drama of the approach. To comply with safety regulations, the National Trust has had to replace it with a wooden railing to protect visitors from the steep drop below – something that was already worrying the future George V when he toured the castle in 1908.

From the Upper Battery, you can see the circular lime kilns, which were an important industry on the island in the late nineteenth century

Lutyens removed the outer wall from the Ramp

THE WALLED GARDEN

The planting for the small walled garden to the north of the castle was designed by Gertrude Jekyll. An early patron of Lutyens, in 1896 she had commissioned him to design her own home, Munstead Wood in Surrey, and as the foremost garden designer of her time, she collaborated with him on a number of country house garden projects. As she had first introduced Lutyens to Hudson, and designed the garden for his house at Deanery Garden, it was natural that she should also be consulted about Lindisfarne.

In May 1906 Jekyll took the train north to Lindisfarne, accompanied by Lutyens, a cantankerous raven called Black Jack and a large bag of pep-

Gertrude Jekyll, who designed the planting for the Walled Garden. Hudson publicised this portrait in Country Life *shortly after it was painted by William Nicholson in 1920 (National Portrait Gallery, London)*

permint bull's-eyes. Already a large woman, she was gingerly hoisted into a small boat by Hudson's manservant and rowed over to Holy Island. She made an initial survey, and Hudson had flowers planted among the rocks beneath the castle in 1906 and 1908, but it was not until 1911 that her planting plans were implemented. Hudson had wanted to create a water garden in the boggy area immediately to the north of the castle known as the Stank in the hope that it 'might attract a few birds'. He also envisaged a walled croquet lawn and tennis court. However, Lutyens's ambitious initial scheme proved too expensive, so Hudson settled for replanting the existing modest walled garden, which had hitherto probably been used only to grow vegetables for the garrison. It was set on a sheltered, southward-facing slope 500 metres to the north of the castle and visible from the main bedroom windows. Curiously, this was very much in the Northumberland tradition: Wallington and many other houses in these parts have walled gardens in sheltered spots some distance away.

The walls and paving were laid in the spring of 1911. Within them, Gertrude Jekyll devised borders filled with plants that would flower in summer, when Hudson was staying in the castle. On one side roses were to be planted. On the other, espalier fruit trees, vegetables and herbs: 'I can sow mint, thyme, sage, sorrel, chives, savory', she recorded in her notebook. In the garden were also to be gladioli, fuchsias, hollyhocks, mallows, sunflowers and Japanese anemones plus cottage garden plants in the central beds. The National Trust is re-creating the Jekyll scheme, following her original plans.

(Right) The Walled Garden

HOLY ISLAND

Beblowe Crag, on which Lindisfarne Castle stands, is quite unlike the rest of the island – a 30-metre-high tooth of bare rock protruding from flat pasture land. Geology is the reason: it was formed when a cone of molten dolerite (known locally as whinstone) forced its way through a crack in the surrounding limestone.

In 635 St Aidan was summoned from Iona by King Oswald of Northumbria to found a monastic community on this remote spot. ('Farne' comes from the Celtic *fahren*, 'a place of retreat'.) If Lindisfarne had been a Mediterranean island, he would have built his church up on the crag, but this is Northumberland, and he sensibly chose more sheltered ground on the south-west corner of the island, away from the North Sea gales.

Aidan was succeeded in 685 by St Cuthbert, who had reluctantly agreed to exchange his bleak hermitage on the Inner Farne for a bishop's mitre. Cuthbert's holy life and the discovery of his miraculously preserved body inspired the creation of the Lindisfarne Gospels and transformed the island into a place of pilgrimage. But the growing wealth of the monastery also made it a target. From Beblowe Crag the worried monks could have watched the smoke rising from their farms on the mainland, as first Danish Vikings, and then the marauding Scots, pillaged the coastland opposite. In 793 the church itself was gutted by 'the heathen'. The last Danish raid, in 875, drove out the monks, who carried with them the precious relics of St Aidan and St Cuthbert and the Lindisfarne Gospels on a journey that was to last seven years.

In 1082 a party of Benedictine monks from Durham Cathedral, where St Cuthbert's relics had finally come to rest, returned to the island. Fifty years later, they refounded the Priory church on its old site, christening Lindisfarne 'Holy Island' in Cuthbert's memory. The Priory ruins are now in the care of English Heritage. Despite the continuing threat from the Scots, Beblowe Crag seems to have remained unfortified.

The opening page of St Matthew's Gospel, from the Lindisfarne Gospels (now in the British Library). They were illuminated by a monk named Eadfrith about 698

(Right) King Egfrid trying to persuade Cuthbert to leave his hermitage on the Inner Farne and become bishop of Lindisfarne; painted by William Bell Scott in 1856 for Wallington

KING ECGFRID AND BISHOP TRUMWINE
PERSUADE CUTHBERT TO BE MADE
BISHOP. DCLXXXIV.

THE TUDOR FORT

When Henry VIII dissolved Lindisfarne Priory and the other medieval monasteries in 1537, he inherited the problem of dealing with the Border forays. An Order in Council decreed that all 'Havens should be fensed with bulwarks and blockehouses against the Scots'. In 1543 Edward Seymour, Lord Hertford was despatched with a formidable punitive expedition against the Scots, because of their continuing devastation of the border counties and of their new alliance with the French. The value of the harbour at Holy Island was soon demonstrated, for Lord Hertford landed over 2,000 troops on his way to Berwick, and ten English warships anchored in the haven.

The first serious attempt at fortification had taken place the previous year. Robert Rooke of Berwick planned two bulwarks – one to command the road and the other to defend the island. 'There is', he reported, 'stone plentie and sufficient remayning of the olde abbey lately dissolved.' In 1548/9 Thomas Holcroft and an engineer were directed to 'view the place by the churche, what hill or grounde were mete for fortification there'. The reconnaissance must have been quickly followed by actual building, probably by Thomas Gower, the surveyor of works at Berwick, for in the Border Survey made in 1550, Sir Robert Bowes reported: 'The forte of Beblowe, within the Holy Island, lyeth very well for the defence of the haven there.' He argued the need for the fort:

The Holy Island is a place much necessarye to be defended and preserved, for there is a harboroughe sufficient for a great navye of shippes to rest safely in, and very aptlye for the warrs towards Scotland. And in that Island be both store houses, brewe

houses, and backe houses, to conserve and prepare victualls sufficient to furnish the said navye withall; which storehouses must either contynuallye be kept in reparations, or ells they will shortelye decaye.

The Priory church became a naval storehouse protected by the garrison.

A survey carried out in 1561 described the fort on Beblowe Crag as 'nothing but a highe Rocke and a platteforame made on the toppe, and a vamure [wall] therof beinge of turf which ys nowe consumed awaye'. Queen Elizabeth, no doubt mindful of the threat of invasion from the north, dispatched engineers in 1570 to deal with the dilapidated platform. This time the work was properly funded and thoroughly done over two years. The restored fort proved more resilient and was defended by the artillery of the day – culverins and demi-culverins, sakers and falcons; but it was never to be tested by siege.

With the accession of James I in 1603, England and Scotland were united under one king, and the fort, and the harbour which it guarded, lost their importance. However, the garrison, which had in 1559 consisted of a captain, two master gunners (on 1s per day), one master's mate (on 10d), and twenty soldiers (on 8d), remained at this strength for at least another 80 years.

In 1635 Sir William Brereton, the Parliamentary general, visited the island and recorded that: 'In a dainty little fort there lives Captain Rugg, governor of the fort, who is as famous for his generous and free entertainment of strangers as for his great bottle nose, which is the largest I have seen. There are neat, warm, and convenient rooms in this little fort.' Four years later, Charles I made an expedition to the North. Twenty ships under the command of the Marquess of Hamilton anchored in the harbour and landed two regiments of

(Left) The stone stairway to the Upper Battery was part of the original fort

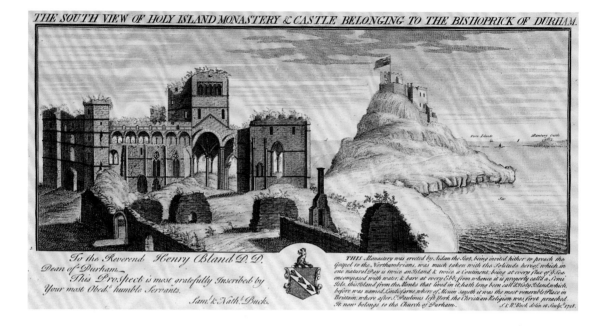

THE SOUTH VIEW OF HOLY ISLAND MONASTERY & CASTLE BELONGING TO THE BISHOPRICK OF DURHAM.

The ruins of Lindisfarne Priory, with the fort beyond, in 1728; engraving by Samuel and Nathaniel Buck

foot, which marched towards Berwick. One of the King's suite, John Aston, a gentleman from Cheshire, wrote in his diary of a visit to the island:

There is a pretty fort in it, which upon this occasion was repaired and put into forme. There are two batteries on it, on the lower stood mounted three iron peeces and two of brasse, with carriadges and platformes in good order. On the higher was one brasse gunne and two iron ones with all ammunition to them.

Once again, Captain Rugg and his celebrated nose was mentioned. Yet another visitor at this time, Father Gilbert Blakhal, a Roman Catholic missionary to Scotland whose ship was driven into the harbour by a great storm of 1643, also wrote of a visit to the governor, the same Captain Rugg and 'his great nose'.

Rugg was clearly a character. He wrote a rhyming letter to King Charles I, beginning:

Where Lindisfarne and Holy Island stand,
These worthless lines sends to your worthie hands

and went on to petition for sixteen months' arrears of pay, the lack of which had left him owing many bills. He ended:

And that greate God that houlds the devell
    in fetters,
Blesse good King Charles, my self and you my
    debtors.

He signed himself:

The great commander of the Gormorants
The Geese and Ganders of these Hallowed lands.

Rugg was not to be commander much longer, for in 1645 a Colonel Shafto was apparently the Governor. The House of Commons in that year adopted a resolution that lands and estates on the mainland opposite Holy Island belonging to Colonel Thomas Haggerston, a Royalist and prisoner of the Parliamentary forces, should be sold, and the proceeds used for the payment of arrears of pay due to Shafto and his soldiers. In addition, £100 was to be paid to Captain Rugg, late Captain of the Island, 'for his relief, he having first rendered it into the hands of Parliament'. Debt-ridden Captain Rugg never received his dubious reward, for he died a year later and his will included a legacy to his daughter of the £100 owed to him by

Parliament. The garrison appears not to have been paid any of the sums due until ten years later, and then only as a result of litigation by Colonel Shafto's widow.

Captain Batton became Governor after Shafto, and a 'considerable force' was sent to Holy Island in 1646 by order of the House of Commons, because 'it was of such consequence to the Northern parts of the kingdom'. In 1647, after Berwick fell to the Royalists, Batton was solicited by Sir Marmaduke Langdale:

If you please to consider the ends being changed, perhaps, for which you first engaged, and comply with the King's interest, by keeping the fort now in possession for the King's use, I will engage myself to see all the arrears due to yourself and the soldiers duly paid, and to procure his Majesty's favour for the future.

Batton refused and was formally thanked by the House of Commons.

A year later he wrote to the Earl of Manchester, Speaker of the House of Lords: he had been in a besieged condition nearly six weeks; the enemy had made a garrison at Haggerston House, within two miles of the island, and were preventing relief reaching the poor inhabitants and the garrison, 'who for fear of attack are put to an extraordinary duty and are in want of provisions and money'; the

The castle from the north-east, by John Varley (Laing Art Gallery, Newcastle upon Tyne)

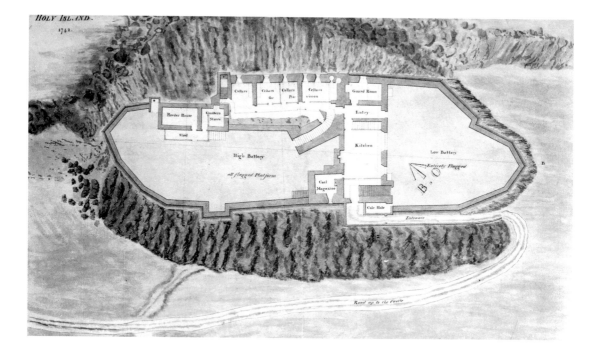

Plan of the castle in 1742

Scots had taken over Berwick by agreement with the Royalists. Could not, he begged, a ship or two be sent to his assistance, 'that he may be able to give the better account of that his frontier garrison, which is of great concernment to that part of the country?' Relief, with 'necessaries', was brought by Colonel Fenwick's Horse, and some dragoons.

In 1649 the situation seemed just as precarious, for Batton had to send his wife to Newcastle carrying the warning that without immediate supplies he might be forced to deliver up the castle. A force under Major John Meyer set off with all possible speed, beat off the enemy's guard and delivered provisions for six months.

After this, the garrison appears not to have been under threat, and records relate mainly to building and repairs. In 1683 Martin Beckman, the King's Second Engineer, made a 'Ground Plott of Holy Island', including a detailed ground plan of the castle, with a view to further improvements. He also illustrated a second small fort, which had been constructed in 1675 at the east end of the Heugh, the cliff to the south of the Priory. On the survey

drawing this fort is described as a 'Plattforme and Redoutte made and designed by Dan: Collingwood Esquire and Mr Robt Trollopp'. Trollope, who originally came from York, was the architect of the Exchange and Guildhall in Newcastle, as well as Capheaton Hall in Northumberland, which he designed for Sir John Swinburne. His fort at Lindisfarne was unfortunately allowed to fall into ruins after it was built, and only fragments now remain.

By 1715, the garrison on Holy Island had been reduced to seven men. In that year the peace of the castle was disturbed by a few hours of drama. Lancelot Errington, the master of a brigantine at anchor in the harbour, paid a visit to the master-gunner (an amateur barber) ostensibly to be shaved. He returned a little later with his nephew, Mark, pretending to have lost his watch. They threatened the master-gunner with pistols, and crying 'Damn you, the Castle is our own', ejected him and the only other soldier on duty. The Old Pretender's flag was unfurled above the castle, and for a night the two men were able to savour a brief taste of Jacobite glory, but next day their signals to the mainland went unanswered, and the fort was quickly recaptured by a party of soldiers from Berwick, who took them prisoner. Later they contrived to burrow their way out of Berwick gaol and, after spending nine days hidden in a pea stack near Bamburgh Castle, managed to escape.

In 1742 Captain Thomas Phillips drew a plan of the castle, which shows an L-shaped layout very similar to what we see today. By the 1770s, the fortress was said to be 'of little more service than to add to the national debt'. The military garrison had its guns withdrawn in 1819 during the civil unrest which followed the Napoleonic Wars. This proved a temporary measure, for, as the Rev. W. W. Keeling reported, 'a few years later some old muzzles were seen again over its walls'. These were removed in 1882 to make way for 156 barrels of gunpowder and three 64-pounders, the castle's last and grandest armament, with a range sufficient to threaten any hostile approach to the haven. For just over a decade the fort was manned by a Volunteer Coast Artillery detachment, which finally withdrew in 1893. From then on, coast-guards seem to have used the buildings occasionally, while the island began to prosper on profits derived from limestone quarrying, the herring fisheries, farming, and – not least – holidaymakers. Among those attracted to the island, in July 1901, was the Scottish architect Charles Rennie Mackintosh, who drew the gaunt and towering walls of the castle – so similar to the south façade of Glasgow School of Art, the first phase of which he had just completed.

The castle from the south-west, sketched by Charles Rennie Mackintosh in 1901, shortly before Hudson acquired it

(Overleaf) Lindisfarne from the west with remains of the limeworks jetty

THE EDWARDIAN HOUSE

'Have got Lindisfarne.' With these words Edward Hudson summoned Edwin Lutyens to Holy Island in January 1902. 'Ramparts and three miles from land!' was the architect's enthusiastic response.

The previous summer, Hudson and Peter Anderson Graham, later the editor of *Country Life*, had been on holiday in the area when they came on the deserted castle. Intrigued, they scaled the wall and looked inside. The coastguards had left the interior in disorder and squalor, with broken furniture and crockery still littering the floor, but Hudson saw the possibilities and took a lease on the castle from the Crown. He had grown up in a drab villa in Notting Hill and had the city-dweller's idealised view of country life. Here was a chance to live the rural dream that his magazine promoted so successfully. Even before restoration had started, Hudson was planning to invite 30 guests to 'picnic' in the empty castle over Christmas – an idea that Lutyens found delightful, his guests less so.

Lutyens, then 33, had established himself as the leading country house architect of his day. The early 'Surrey picturesque' period with which he had made his reputation was now behind him; and he had begun to show his virtuosity in designs for houses all over the country, adopting a variety of styles, eclectic, yet original and personal, with a sympathetic feeling for texture and respect for local materials. Much of his work to date had involved adaptation, addition and alteration of existing buildings, and the castle cannot have posed exceptional problems for him. He excelled at romantic reconstructions of this sort.

Lutyens's task was to fit a modern holiday home within the Tudor ramparts. The outer walls were strong, but functional rather than ornamental, and the inner buildings were neglected, but still standing. A shallow stone ramp, traversing the southern flank of the crag, gave access to the castle's only outer door; through this, steps at right angles led to a terrace or Lower Battery (see plan on the inside front cover). Lutyens retained this approach (although he removed the ramp's stone balustrade), and partly rebuilt the block of buildings at the western side of the battery to include a notable Entrance Hall and Kitchen, with bedrooms above, and with generous mullioned windows overlooking the North Sea. Running west from this new

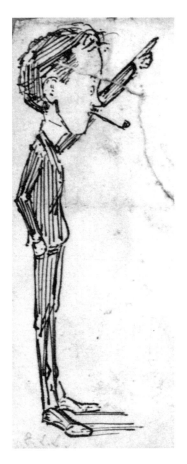

A caricature of Lutyens in 1906, when he was working on Lindisfarne

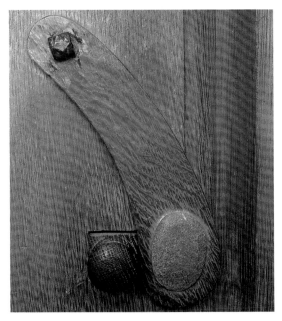

Lutyens paid great attention to details like this lead-weighted door latch

The castle about 1906, before Lutyens had added the North Bedrooms range

Entrance Hall, and at a slightly lower level, were two dark, stone-vaulted chambers which now became the principal living-rooms, with altered windows and new fireplaces – the Dining Room and the Ship Room. From the Hall, the old stairway to the Upper Battery was retained, and an angled flight of stairs was added, leading off it to a new Long Gallery, slightly tapered, with windows facing south on to the Upper Battery, and with a large fireplace at the far end. Along the north side of this gallery, on the site of a third battery (known as the Queen's), he later introduced three new bedrooms, below whose tiny windows the rock fell sheer.

Part of the old West Guardhouse, which had contained the Governor's living quarters, was demolished, and from the remainder Lutyens made two bow-windowed bedrooms, one above the other, overlooking the mainland, and with access from the Long Gallery. Altogether, four living-

Lutyens hung the curtains on rods that swing away from the windows to reveal the neo-Gothic tracery he had inserted

rooms and nine bedrooms were made, with one bathroom. At this date, Lutyens still expected his clients to wash in hip-baths and basins, with hot water brought up by servants. Another bathroom was created much later.

Lutyens created an L-shaped house which linked the castle's old east and west buildings. The changed architectural details were both significant and sympathetic. Photographs taken at the end of the nineteenth century show that the 'pretty fort' did not really have the fairytale appearance of Finden's engravings of the 1830s, with their romantic cluster of towers and turrets. Its appearance was in reality more severe. Lutyens simplified the silhouette, rounded the edges and removed the battlements. The new, taut outlines of the castle seemed to spring logically from the naked rock.

Work began in May 1903 and was not completed until July 1906; the Long Gallery bedrooms were added in 1912. There was no electricity or gas, and lighting was provided by quantities of candles. It was, however, a house occupied mostly in the summer, so the candles were not needed until the evenings, and great log fires more or less kept the chill at bay. Lutyens designed some of the oak furniture for the castle, and his hand is apparent in the inventiveness and finish

Lutyens's Castle Drogo in Devon (1910–30) shows his ability to reinterpret the castle form in new ways

The curved steps subtly echo the double arches in the Long Gallery

of the woodwork, exemplified by the door latches and bolts, the panelling and details of beams and architraves. The rest of the furniture, mainly seventeenth-century English and Flemish oak, was chosen by Hudson and Lutyens.

Lindisfarne was Lutyens's first castle. Two more followed – Lambay Castle off the coast of Dublin (1905) and Castle Drogo in Devon (1910–30), which is also in the care of the National Trust. Neither is exactly comparable, for Lambay was to a great extent a new construction, and Drogo entirely so. But they all show Lutyens's command of the medieval architectural vernacular without recourse to detailed imitation. The architectural writer Christopher Hussey called the style of his work at Lindisfarne 'Romance without period'. The same phrase could apply to Lambay and Drogo. All three demonstrated Lutyens's fondness for subtle combinations of building materials – stone, brick, slate and cobble; in all three, he created an atmospheric interior from stone, sturdy columns and rounded arches, spiral stairs, great fireplaces and leaded windows; in all three, he

made dramatic use of the irregular rise and fall of levels, of angled building patterns, and of a poetic relationship and contrast between stone walls, grassland and skyline.

Before Lindisfarne, Lutyens had already designed one house for Hudson, Deanery Garden at Sonning in Berkshire, completed in 1901. Several pieces of the furniture now at Lindisfarne came from there. Other commissions followed, including new offices for *Country Life* in 1904. The two men, sensitive, sentimental and shy, became lifelong friends. There is no doubt that Lutyens was assisted in his career by Hudson's unreserved admiration and by the articles which were published in *Country Life* about his principal buildings. They were constantly together. Lutyens had a standing invitation to dine at Hudson's London house in Queen Anne's Gate; and Hudson accompanied the Lutyenses to the opening of New Delhi in 1931. Lutyens's wife Emily described him exclaiming with tears of pride: 'Poor old Christopher Wren! *He* could never have done this!'

The mass of the castle appears particularly stark from the north-east

(Right) Barbie Lutyens in the Long Gallery in 1910

LIFE AT LINDISFARNE

'I want to amuse myself with the place.'
Edward Hudson on Lindisfarne, 1902

Hudson was an enigma, a man of few words and almost no small talk. Like many shy people, he seemed to get on best with children. Lutyens's daughter Mary remembered him as 'a tall man, very kind, but unattractively plain':

He was very good-natured. We had a fire-screen in the nursery, the bottom part of which could be moved up leaving a gap at the bottom. It was perfect for playing French Revolutions, and Hudson was most obliging in kneeling on the floor and putting his head through the gap so that we could guillotine him.

Lutyens's children became a surrogate family for the bachelor Hudson, who commissioned a series of atmospheric photographs of them at Lindisfarne from the *Country Life* photographer Charles Latham. Despite his diffidence, Hudson loved entertaining, and Lindisfarne became the setting for a series of summer house parties, to which he invited a wide range of guests, including the ballerina Alicia Markova, the conductor Sir Malcolm Sargent, and Elizabeth von Arnim, author of *Elizabeth and her German Garden* (1898). From 1906 the castle was also open to the public: 'A small charge of 6d is made for admission.'

The grandest visitors were the Prince and Princess of Wales (the future George V and Queen Mary), who toured the castle in July 1908. Hudson was rigid with nerves, and the occasion was not a success. According to Lutyens, who was staying at the time, the royal party arrived in a procession of

eight carriages: 'The Prince was awfully bored apparently with the lecture given by some archae-ologist – Hodges – and looked at his watch every two minutes'. Lutyens did not help matters by explaining the castle's drainage system. The Prince responded, 'oh yes, drains, of course drains', with-out a smile:

He was terribly alarmed at the gangway up and wanted a wall built. I told him we had pulled one down and that if he really thought it unsafe we would put nets out. He thought that very funny.

The Princess couldn't bear the cobbles, they hurt her feet. I told her we were very proud of them! ... The Prince was awfully anxious to get away when he found the tide was rising, for a sailor I thought him over nervous.

Among the more frequent and exotic of Hud-son's visitors was the Portuguese cellist Madame Guilhermina Suggia. The *Country Life* writer Avray Tipping thought she looked like a jaguar. Lytton Strachey, who stayed at Lindisfarne in September 1918, was another to fall under her spell:

She is very attractive, owing I think chiefly to (1) great simplicity – not a trace of the airs & graces of the "Diva" with a European reputation – no bother about playing or not playing – almost a boyishness at times; and (2) immense vitality – her high spirits enormous, and almost unceasing ... I suppose, beside this, that she is a flirt ... Then in the evening after dinner she gave her full dress performances. It was really all an extraordinary joy.

Something of her high spirits is captured in Augustus John's famous portrait, in which she is shown playing Bach on the Stradivarius given her by Hudson.

Strachey was less impressed with Hudson ('a pathetically dreary figure – so curiously repulsive, too, and so, somehow, lost ... A kind of bourgeois gentilhomme also') and his castle:

A poor affair – except for the situation, which is magnificent, and the great foundations and massive battlements, whence one has amazing prospects of sea, hills, other castles, etc. – extraordinarily roman-tic – on every side. But the building itself is all timid Lutyens – very dark, with nowhere to sit, and nothing but stone under, over & round you, which produces a distressing effect – especially when one's hurrying downstairs late for dinner – to slip would be instant death. No – not a comfortable place, by any means.

Emily Lutyens, who did not get on with Hudson, also had reservations about the castle. She came away from a family holiday there in October 1906, appalled by the cold, by the way the fires and candles smoked from the north-east wind, and by the castle's unsuitability for mischievous children.

But others loved the place. In 1909, while in his final year at Eton, Billy Congreve caught diphtheria. He was the youngest son of Hudson's friends, General Sir Walter Congreve, who had won the VC in the Boer War, and his wife, Celia La Touche, who was to win the Croix de Guerre while nursing on the Western Front during the First World War. Billy had been on many happy family holidays to Lindisfarne, and returned here to convalesce for two months. Hudson said of him, 'That boy has quality', and planned to bequeath the castle to him. (He had earlier proposed to Billy's aunt and had been rejected.) But Billy Congreve had inherited his parents' courage. In the First World War, he won the MC, the DSO and, finally, on the Somme in July 1916, while tending the wounded under heavy fire, a posthumous VC – the first soldier to be awarded all three of these medals for gallantry. Lutyens designed his memorial plaque.

Hudson's flamboyant friend Madame Suggia playing the cello he gave her; painted by Augustus John in 1920–3 at Hudson's suggestion (Tate Gallery)

(Far left) Edward Hudson at Lindisfarne

LATER HISTORY

Hudson bought the freehold to the castle only in 1918, but without an heir and too busy in London to make regular trips north, he decided in 1921 to sell. The price was £25,000 and the purchaser Oswald Falk, a London stockbroker and friend of the economist Maynard Keynes. Like Keynes, 'Foxy' Falk was both an important figure in the City of London and a great lover of the arts, patronising the ballet and collecting Cézanne watercolours and Mexican sculpture, besides much else.

After only a few years, Falk sold the castle to Sir Edward de Stein, a very successful merchant

The Lilburns in the Kitchen

banker whose business merged with Lazards in 1960. He was a man of many talents – pianist, landscape gardener, watercolourist, 'enthusiastic but somewhat inaccurate birdwatcher', writer of light verse, collector of porcelain, and generous supporter of Toc H and the London boys' club movement. He never married, and so encouraged his sister Gladys to use Lindisfarne as a family home, for the school holidays of nephews and nieces. He was also happy to lend it to friends, for weekends and honeymoons. But especially it was a children's summer holiday place. For what could be more delightful than to spend days bathing and sailing, mackerel fishing and lobster-potting, walking and bird-watching; what better than to sleep in a real castle and to wake in the morning to a view only equalled by the look-out in the crow's-nest of a sailing ship?

Sir Edward gave the castle to the National Trust in 1944, and remained as its tenant until he died in 1965. His sister Gladys took over the tenancy until her death three years later. During these years domestic continuity was maintained first by Mr and Mrs Jack Lilburn, whom Hudson had installed in the castle as caretakers, and in subsequent years by their son and daughter, who retired in 1968.

In 1965 Lindisfarne formed the backdrop to one of the more unusual films shot in an English country house – Roman Polanski's thriller *Cul-de-Sac*, which featured a shaven-headed Donald Pleasence in a nightie and the French actress Françoise Dorléac running naked along the beach on a distinctly chilly January day. Life at Lindisfarne has been quieter since.

Lionel Stander doing a handstand on the Lower Battery during the filming of Roman Polanski's Cul-de-Sac. *Donald Pleasence sits in the rocking chair*

BIBLIOGRAPHY

Gertrude Jekyll's plans for the Walled Garden are in the Reef Point Collection, University of California at Berkeley. Lytton Strachey's letter is among the Hutchinson Papers in the Harry Ransom Humanities Research Center, University of Texas at Austin.

ANON., *Northumberland County History*, 1895.

ASLET, Clive, *The Last Country Houses*, London, 1982.

BAKER, David, 'Lutyens at Lindisfarne', unpublished B. Arch. thesis, Newcastle University, 1975.

BLAKHAL, G., *A Brieffe Narration*, 1666.

BRERETON, William, *Notes on a Journey through Durham and Northumberland in the Year 1635*, Newcastle, 1844.

BROWN, Jane, *Lutyens and the Edwardians*, London, 1996.

BUTLER, A. S. G., *The Architecture of Sir Edwin Lutyens*, London, 1950.

COLVIN, H. M., ed., *The History of the King's Works, Volume IV, 1485–1600 (Part II)*, London, 1982, pp. 674–9.

CORNFORTH, John, *The Inspiration of the Past*, Harmondsworth, 1985.

FESTING, Sally, *Gertrude Jekyll*, London, 1991.

[GRAHAM, Peter Anderson], 'Lindisfarne Castle, Northumberland', *Country Life*, 7 June 1913, pp. 830–42.

HODGSON, John, *A History of Northumberland*, 1820.

HOLROYD, Michael, *Lytton Strachey*, London, 1968; 1976 edn, pp. 744–7.

HUSSEY, Christopher, *The Life of Sir Edwin Lutyens*, London, 1950.

KEELING, W. W. F., 'Lindisfarne or Holy Island: Its History and Associations', *Newcastle Daily Journal*, 1883.

The upturned boats below the castle have been converted into huts

LUTYENS, Mary, *Edwin Lutyens*, London, 1991.

MACKENZIE, Eneas, *An Historical, Topographical and Descriptive View of the County of Northumberland*, Newcastle, 1825.

MAUDE, Pamela, 'Portrait of a Perfectionist: Edward Hudson, the Founder of "Country Life"', *Country Life*, 12 January 1967, pp. 58–60.

OLIVER, Stephen, *Rambles in Northumberland and the Scottish Borders*, London, 1835.

PERCY, Clayre, and RIDLEY, Jane, ed., *The Letters of Edwin Lutyens*, London, 1985.

PERRY, Richard, *A Naturalist on Lindisfarne*, London, 1946.

RAINE, James, *The History and Antiquities of North-Durham*, London, 1852.

ROBSON, D., *A Guide to the Geology of Northumberland and the Borders*, 1966.

SAUNDERS, Andrew, *Fortress Britain*, Liphook, 1989.

SCOTT, Walter, *The Border Antiquities of England and Scotland*, London, 1814.

TINNISWOOD, Adrian, *Historic Houses of the National Trust*, London, 1991, pp. 262–7.

TOMLINSON, William Weaver, *Comprehensive Guide to the County of Northumberland*, London, 1888.

TOOLEY, Michael and Rosanna, *The Gardens of Gertrude Jekyll in Northern England*, Witton-le-Wear, 1982.

WHITE, Walter, *Northumberland and the Border*, London, 1859.

The National Trust
for Places of Historic Interest or Natural Beauty

Legacies

Have you ever considered leaving a charitable bequest in your Will? Whatever their size, legacies are vital to the National Trust. They are the second largest source of income for the Trust, and we could not survive without them. They are used to fund major restoration projects, to acquire and endow new properties around the country, or for any other area of the Trust's work that you may wish to specify. **They are not spent on administration costs.**

Remembering the National Trust with a legacy may also prevent your estate from paying Inheritance Tax and will at the same time help to maintain the special heritage of England, Wales and Northern Ireland for future generations.

A free booklet is available providing helpful advice on will-making in general, as well as suggested wording, should you wish to support the National Trust in some way.

For your copy or for further information, please contact the Legacies Office,
36 Queen Anne's Gate, London SW1H 9AS; telephone 020 7222 9251 (minicom 0870 240 3207)
or e-mail: legacies@nationaltrust.org.uk